DATE DUE

OCT 0 9 2000		
OCT 3 1 2000		
AUG 1 2002		
NOV 2 2002		
NOV 1 7 2003		
MAR 2 3 2005		
FEB 0 3 2007		
MAY 0 3 2010		
MAY 0 1 2010		
JUN 2 9 2011		
MAY 1 3 2013		

looking at art

9

LANDSCAPE
& NATURE

Grolier Educational

SHERMAN TURNPIKE, DANBURY, CONNECTICUT 06816

Grolier Educational
Grolier Publishing Company, Inc.

Grolier Educational Staff
Joseph Tessitore, *Senior Vice President, Sales and Marketing*
Robert B. Hall, *Senior Vice President, Sales*
Beverly A. Balaz, *Vice President, Marketing*
A. Joseph Hollander, *Vice President and Publisher, School and Library Reference*
Molly Stratton, *Editor, School and Library Reference*

This edition first published 1996 by Grolier Educational, Danbury, Connecticut 06816.
Copyright © 1996 Marshall Cavendish Limited.

ISBN 0-7172-7595-7 (set)
ISBN 0-7172 7604-X (volume)

Cataloging information can be obtained directly from Grolier Educational.

Marshall Cavendish Limited
Editorial staff
Series Consultant: Anthea Peppin,
Senior Education Officer, National Gallery, London
Series Editor: Tim Cooke
Editor: Sarah Halliwell
Senior Designer: Wayne Humphries
Picture Rights Coordinators: Vimu Patel, Sophie Mortimer
Text: Alice Peebles
Index: Susan Dawson
Printed in Malaysia

Contents

Early & Renaissance Art

From earliest times, artists around the world have created pictures of the places and events that were important to them. These images often showed the countryside where their community farmed or hunted.

As societies developed, people gathered in larger settlements and eventually in cities. Buildings became grander, and their walls offered ideal surfaces for painting. Wall paintings were popular about 2,000 years ago in ancient Rome. In the *Garden of Livia*, for example, the artist painted a landscape full of birds, fruit trees, and flowers.

After the Romans, there was a gap of some 1,000 years when landscape rarely featured in art in the Western world. In Europe, where Christianity became the official religion, pictures usually featured Mary and Jesus or saints. Rather than showing real scenes, the backgrounds of these paintings were often plain gold.

Filling in the background

The situation began to change in the 14th century. Artists illustrated calendars with scenes of peasants at work in the countryside. The month of August, for example, would be represented by harvesters in a field. In time, such landscape scenes replaced the traditional gold backgrounds.

In Italy at the end of the 15th century, city-states like Florence grew rich and powerful. This coincided with a renewed interest in the arts of ancient times. This exciting period—known as the Renaissance—saw a rapid development of artistic skills through scientific learning and looking at nature. One of the major discoveries was a technique called perspective, which artists used to create an illusion

Garden of Livia: Roman wall painting
Can you see the delicately painted fruits and flowers in the trees in this ancient wall painting?

of distance and depth. Such skills gave Renaissance paintings new realism.

A rocky landscape

Look at Gozzoli's *Journey of the Magi*, painted around 1460, which shows the biblical story of the three kings going to worship the infant Jesus. The painter has given one of the kings the face of his patron, Lorenzo de' Medici; the scene is full of figures from Lorenzo's court. The landscape has a sense of depth, but it is really just a stage across which the procession passes. It is only shown to help tell the story.

The development of techniques such as perspective, however, gave artists fresh new ways of showing the world around them.

Journey of the Magi: Benozzo Gozzoli
Gozzoli tells a traditional tale in a new way, setting a religious story against a colorful natural scene.

The Emperor Ming Huang's Journey in Shu

(ninth century)

After the collapse of the Roman Empire at the end of the fifth century there was little new art in Europe for some 500 years. In China, by contrast, ancient Chinese culture and artistic traditions flourished under the Tang Dynasty from the seventh to the tenth centuries.

The Buddhist religion, which was important in China, stressed the need for people to live in harmony with the natural world. Such beliefs contributed to a new style in landscape painting. Artists showed nature in a perfect rather than a realistic way.

A feeling for nature can be seen in this famous landscape of the late Tang period. Although painted on a single piece of silk, the picture shows three separate stages of the emperor's journey. The Chinese read from the right-hand side of a page to the left—not from left to right, as in English—and you can read this painting in the same way. On the right, the emperor descends the mountains; he rests on the plains and finally ascends more mountains on the left.

The rocks and precipices tower above the travelers amid decorative patterns of swirling clouds. Look back at Gozzoli's picture *(see page 5)*. How do you think this painting is different? Notice how Gozzoli placed his figures at the front of the picture, where they could be recognized: here they are barely visible. To this artist, the landscape and clouds are as important as the imperial procession.

The Effects of Good Government

by Ambrogio Lorenzetti (active 1319–1347)

The Italian city of Siena was at the peak of its power in the 1330s, when Lorenzetti was commissioned to paint the walls of the council room in the new town hall. The artist chose to depict the ideal state that Siena should aim to achieve. His frescoes, or wall paintings, show the differences between well-organized and badly organized societies. Using his knowledge of Siena and the surrounding countryside, Lorenzetti created one of the earliest landscape scenes in European art.

The *Allegory of Good Government*, from which the detail opposite is taken, is 46 feet long. This half depicts a contented and productive countryside; the other half shows the busy and industrious town. On another wall, the artist illustrated the effects of bad government, but that painting is now badly damaged.

The well-run city and fertile countryside work in harmony together. Wealthy citizens on horses ride out from the gate of the walled city for a day's hunting. They pass peasants bringing their produce to market. Can you see the man driving a pig up the hill? In the distance, orderly fields and vineyards cover the land.

Hovering over the city gate is a guardian angel holding the figure of a hanged man. She reminds the town's citizens that in earlier times the region was ravaged by war and civil strife. The dead man is a warning not to return to those violent times.

The Madonna with Chancellor Rolin

by Jan van Eyck (about 1385–1441)

When the powerful politician Chancellor Rolin commissioned van Eyck to paint his portrait in the early 15th century, he wanted to be shown as a man who was both wealthy and pious.

Rolin was a statesman in the Burgundian territories, which fell within parts of present-day Belgium, Holland, and France. His fine clothing shows his wealth. Van Eyck shows his patron holding his hands together, deep in prayer. The Virgin Mary and infant Jesus are seated opposite him, as if they were ordinary people in an everyday scene. Rolin kneels close to Mary, implying he is a good Christian.

Between the two main figures, a carefully painted floor leads your eye out through an arched window to a private flower garden. Here, two figures gaze out at the view, with peacocks standing nearby. Can you see other birds? Look how the painter gives the impression of a bustling town on the banks of the river. This landscape, though imaginary, captures the feel of the countryside around the Meuse River in van Eyck's native Netherlands.

In southern European art at this time landscape was usually only included in a picture as a backdrop to figures. But in the north, painters paid more attention to it: here van Eyck shows every detail. If you look very closely, you can even see people crossing the bridge. Notice how the artist creates a sense of depth by using lighter colors in the distance.

Saint Francis

by Giovanni Bellini (about 1430–1516)

In this painting of Saint Francis, founder of the Franciscan order of friars, Bellini has brought the landscape right to the front of the picture. This saint rejected his father's wealth to live alone in extreme poverty. Look how Bellini paints him in a bare winter landscape to emphasize his sacrifice.

According to Christian history, Saint Francis was so holy that he received the stigmata—the five wounds of the

crucified Christ—on his body. Can you see the marks on the palms of his hands? The thorns, branches, and twisted roots in the picture recall the crown of thorns that Christ wore on the cross. A single jug is a symbol of the saint's frugal lifestyle. On the desk behind him is a Bible and a skull to remind him that death is inevitable.

Nearby a donkey looks on. By the river, a shepherd tends his flock—a traditional symbol of Christ looking after his followers. In the distance lies the city that the fun-loving Francis once enjoyed but has now rejected.

The Rest on the Flight into Egypt

by Lucas Cranach (1472–1553)

In the Bible, Joseph, the earthly father of Jesus, dreamed that King Herod wanted to kill his newborn son. At once Joseph and his family set off for the safety of Egypt.

Cranach, who was born in southern Germany, paints Joseph, Mary, and Jesus in a glade at the edge of a forest. The landscape is more typical of his own homeland than the arid wastes of the Holy Land, so it would have been familiar and appealing to his audience. Cranach depicts the plants of the forest in great detail. He seems proud of his skill: can you see his initials on a rock?

As the holy family had no time to take any food with them, a band of little angels help them gather provisions. One collects water dripping from a rock in a shell, others gather herbs and a small bird for the family to eat. Notice how one offers the infant Jesus some berries. Others play soothing music on pipes to help keep the weary travelers entertained. Did you spot the sleeping angel?

Behind Mary is a rocky hillside that leads to a far-off horizon. Perhaps the artist is suggesting the long journey that still stretches ahead.

The Fall of Icarus

by Pieter Brueghel the Elder (about 1525–1569)

In Greek mythology, an inventor called Daedalus made feather-and-wax wings for himself and his son Icarus so that they could escape from the island where they were imprisoned. But proud young Icarus ignored his father's warning not to fly too near the sun. The wax holding his wings together melted, and he plunged to his death in the sea below.

The Flemish painter Brueghel brought this myth up to date and placed it in the kind of landscape he knew from his local countryside. Sixteenth-century peasants go about their labors, plowing and tending the sheep. Notice the fisherman casting his line at the water's edge. But look how the chief character in the story, Icarus himself, is barely visible. Brueghel paints only the end of the drama. How long did it take you to notice the comical sight of the legs disappearing into the water?

No one in the picture notices the young man falling to his death. The plowman concentrates on guiding the blade of his plow and does not look up. The shepherd gazes into space. The fisherman checks his line. A merchant ship sails on past. Life goes on regardless of Icarus's tragedy.

Brueghel's paintings often had a moral purpose. What do you think his message might have been in this picture? Perhaps he is suggesting that the young man has been too stubborn in disobeying his father. Like the peasants quietly going about their everyday life, maybe he should have been less ambitious and more satisfied with his life.

The Seventeenth & Eighteenth Centuries

Driven by economic changes, the focus of art shifted north from Italy toward the Netherlands, France, and Britain. There, a different type of society created a new audience that demanded a new type of picture.

During the 17th century the growth of trade and industry saw the rise of wealthy merchants in the cities of Europe. In the countryside, a new aristocracy began to take the place of the power of the Church and the monarchy. These people built great mansions and comfortable houses for themselves and wanted paintings for their walls and private galleries. Gradually, religious painting became less important and subjects such as landscapes and portraits became fashionable.

This was especially true in the Netherlands (present-day Holland and Belgium), where artists turned to the countryside for inspiration. The word landscape itself comes from the Dutch *landschap*, which came into popular use about 1600.

The Dutch were interested in landscape painting for a number of reasons. Since the last decades of the 1500s, they had been struggling to throw off the rule of the Spanish, who had dominated them for more than a century. They wanted to govern themselves and practice their Protestant religion. Artists created a new

The Jewish Cemetery:
Jacob van Ruisdael
This mysterious scene is based partly on a real cemetery and partly on imagination.

rural art that reflected the Protestant view that hard work and family life were the most important values.

Views such as those drawn and painted by Jacob van Ruisdael represented an escape from city life, which had become associated with intrigue and corruption. Looking at an idyllic scene like Rubens's *Autumn Landscape with View of Het Steen*, the viewer would have seen a paradise to contrast with the cramped, disease-ridden streets of Amsterdam or Antwerp.

The Italian ideal

In Italy, however, a new "ideal" form of landscape painting grew out of Renaissance art. It showed scenery in a formal manner. Painters came from France and England to study the ruins of ancient Rome. They also read classical poetry, which praised the idea of a rural community of happy laborers.

Artists adopted this idea of a perfect landscape—known as Arcadia in ancient Greece—which came to represent how civilized humanity could shape nature for its own ends. Paintings still included religious or mythological figures, but these were often tiny compared to the landscape around them.

When artists who visited Italy exhibited their work back home, it inspired great interest. Their audience wanted to see these scenes of classical splendor for themselves. It became fashionable for the wealthy to travel abroad on what was called the "grand tour." After seeing the villas and gardens of ancient and Renaissance times, these "tourists" returned home and tried to reproduce the same effects. Under their influence, landscape gardens became popular in northern Europe.

Autumn Landscape with View of Het Steen: Peter Paul Rubens
Rubens bought Het Steen—Stone House—to study landscape and paint in peace.

Hagar & the Angel

by Claude Lorrain (1600–1682)

In an Old Testament story, Hagar, the maid of Abraham's wife Sarah, becomes pregnant. Fleeing from her home in shame, she hides in the wilderness, where an angel comforts her and tells her to return home.

Do you think that Claude was really interested in this story? His scene is dramatic because of the background rather than the small figures in the corner. The story seems like an excuse to paint a landscape.

Claude was born in the French region of Lorraine and originally worked as a pastry cook. It was only when he took a job in the kitchens of a Roman artist that he became fascinated with painting. For years he sketched the Campagna—the name given to the countryside around Rome—and his paintings always echo this landscape, although most of them are imaginary. Claude's tireless observation of nature made him highly skilled in imitating the effects of light.

One of Claude's important contributions was a technique called *repoussoir*, French for "to push back." Look how the dark trees create a frame within the picture that draws you to the light at the center of the canvas. There, the lighter tones of the river and hillside catch the eye and carry you to the horizon. The trees also make the foreground appear as a kind of stage where the drama is enacted.

Mr. & Mrs. Andrews

by *Thomas Gainsborough (1727–1788)*

The recently married Mrs. Andrews sits proudly in an expensive dress with her husband standing casually next to her. He balances his sporting gun under his arm, his obedient dog at his side. It seems like a simple portrait celebrating a wedding. But there is more to this painting by the English artist Thomas Gainsborough.

First, the couple sit off center and share the canvas with the landscape behind them. This implies that it is as least as important as they are. Also, in the 1740s, when the picture was painted, it was traditional to show newlyweds in a pretty garden or park.

Here however we see Mr. Andrews proudly showing off his farm land.

The audience of the time would have read things into the way the cornfield is painted. The wheat is bunched into sheaves, a symbol of fertility—perhaps the couple will soon have a child? Behind the sheaves stretch lines of furrowed stubble. This is a sign that Mr. Andrews owns a seed drill, then the height of farming technology. His gun shows that he shoots game. The animals on his land are as much his property as the crops are.

Blind Man's Buff

by Jean-Honoré Fragonard (1732–1806)

A group of young French aristocrats play and flirt in a landscape that seems like a playground for the very rich. Above them two cypress trees lead the eye up to a thunderous sky. In this painting there is no hint that there are poor or lonely people in society. This is a carefree world that the playful aristocrats would have liked to be a reality.

Fragonard himself came from a humble background in the south of France. His hometown was Grasse, which is today world-famous for perfume. When he was six, his family moved to Paris, and as a young man he took a job as a clerk in a lawyer's office. But one day he was caught sketching at his desk by his boss and was immediately fired.

With the help of his mother, Fragonard began to study painting. He was so good at it that he won a scholarship to the art school in Rome. There he loved to sit and sketch in the garden of the Villa d'Este, which lay in Tivoli, just outside the city. Even after he returned to Paris, he still composed his paintings with the villa's elegant gardens in mind.

Fragonard was a fine draftsman, which means that he was good at drawing. He observed nature closely, and studied the works of great landscape artists such as Ruisdael (*see page 18*). But although Fragonard's landscapes look like safe wonderlands, the nobility was not to be protected from the outside world for much longer. The French Revolution exploded just 15 years after Fragonard painted this scene, sweeping away the people he served, and the often frivolous art that they had favored.

The Nineteenth Century

As large numbers of people moved to cities looking for work, they became more cut off from the countryside than earlier generations had been. Artists reflected the new perceptions of landscape that this change brought.

During the 18th century most artists painted either natural, pleasant landscapes or those shaped by humankind. But the chaotic period that followed the French Revolution in 1789 had a great impact on painters in all parts of Europe.

The Revolution unleashed a storm of violence. To some artists the world too seemed a place of dramatic forces beyond human control or understanding. This view became the main theme of what is called Romantic art.

The wild side of life

Artists began to show the wild and dangerous side of nature. Instead of sleepy pastures and pretty gardens, they painted bleak moorlands and majestic mountains. The chief Romantic was a German, Caspar David Friedrich. His *Wanderer Looking over a Sea of Fog* sets a solitary man against the vastness and power of nature. The artist seems to ask, "Who can understand this mystery?"

As the century progressed, developments in science and ideas influenced landscape painting. Railroads made traveling easier so people could take

Wanderer Looking over a Sea of Fog: Caspar David Friedrich
The artist wrote: "I have to stay alone in order to fully contemplate and feel nature."

a greater interest in the natural world. It became hard for painters to depict gentle pastoral scenes when society was racing toward the modern age.

Photography also presented artists with a new challenge. The French painters known as the Impressionists tried to capture a specific moment, as in a snapshot. They were interested in what they saw rather than what they already thought about nature.

Painting outdoors

It became easier for artists to paint out of doors. Manufactured paint was now sold in tubes, paints were cheaper to buy, and there was a wider choice of colors available. Artists such as Monet (*see page 33*) captured the color and light of the natural world. They painted whole canvases outdoors, away from their artificially lit studios. This gave their paintings a fresh, new, and airy atmosphere.

Later, artists began to put more personal emotion into their pictures. This resulted in very original images of nature. Van Gogh's *Cornfield and Cypresses* shows his strong feelings for the landscape of the south of France. The bold color and swirling lines make this scene vibrant, but also reveal the painter's troubled mind.

Cornfield and Cypresses:
Vincent van Gogh
Van Gogh was fascinated by the flamelike shapes of cypress trees in southern France.

The Haywain

by John Constable (1776–1837)

Only a dog looks up as an empty haywain, or farm wagon, slowly crosses the Stour River in eastern England, heading to the meadow beyond. If you look closely, you can see a fisherman on the bank to the right. Smoke rises from the chimney of a homey white cottage, while in the distant meadow farmhands in white shirts load hay onto a second wagon.

Can you guess what time of the day it is? When Constable exhibited this painting in 1821, he called it *Land-*

scape: Noon. It shows a peaceful scene during the hay-making season, in a spot that Constable knew well—the shallow part of the river by a local farmer's cottage. Constable was concerned that the details of this scene be accurate, so he made lots of sketches, including a lively and spontaneous full-size oil study. He painted the final picture back in his London studio during the winter of 1820.

But there is more to this painting than a pretty cottage and wagon. Constable's true subject is the landscape and the changing effects of English weather. He observed the sky closely, painting many detailed studies of clouds and carefully noting the exact time of day. In this way he captured the shifting summer clouds, which throw patches of shadow across the green fields. Perhaps the darker clouds on the left warn that a storm is brewing, which will dramatically alter this peaceful scene.

Look at the tree in the center. Constable captures the effects of sunlight shining through the leaves by using thick layers of green and yellow paint, which he spread on with a palette knife. Can you see how the red of the horses' harnesses stands out against the darker colors?

Norham Castle, Sunrise

by J.M.W. Turner (1775–1851)

Somewhere in the hazy blue center of this canvas is a castle perched on a hill. Delicate lemon yellow patches in the sky above suggest the early morning sun. Below the castle the sunlight is reflected in the still waters of the Tweed, a river that flows between England and Scotland. Can you see how Turner has painted reddish-brown shapes to suggest drinking cattle standing in the river? Everything seems dissolved in the soft light. Turner combines

these subtle images to create one of the most atmospheric landscapes in 19th-century painting.

Even though this painting has the subtle look of a watercolor, it is actually painted in oil. Turner usually prepared his canvases with a thick layer of white paint to make the surface smooth. He would then build up layer upon layer of paint. The colors beneath would show through the covering layers, giving the impression of glowing light shining from within the painting. Turner was especially fond of using chrome yellow, which helped him to create this effect.

But Turner, always a private man, was secretive about most of his painting methods. Even in later life, when he had become famous, Turner still preferred to avoid attention and sometimes even traveled under a false name. He often visited Europe, seeking out solitary and dramatic views in his dedication to capturing the effects of light on the landscape.

His painting was so far in advance of his time that it was often criticized as looking crude. Some people even considered his use of brilliant yellow to be shocking. But his admirers claimed that he was a genius. Who do you think was right?

Poppy Field

by Claude Monet (1840–1926)

When a French art critic saw one of Monet's paintings at an exhibition in 1874, he wrote a review mocking it. He described it as crude and unfinished, giving just the "impression" of the subject rather than the real thing. Instead of being upset by the insult, Monet and his fellow painters adopted it and began to call themselves Impressionists. Landscape painting had already become less formal than in previous centuries. Now these French artists introduced a light and "open-air" feel to landscape.

In *Poppy Field*, Monet's wife Camille and young son Jean are walking at the top of a meadow. Monet captures

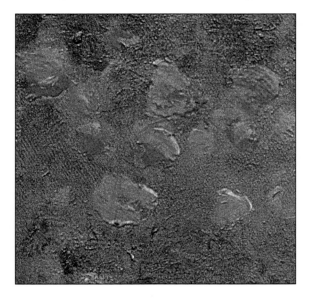

the form of their hats and clothes without painting them in precise detail. Can you see how he uses dabs of red paint on a green background to depict the poppies? At the bottom of the canvas the painter makes the impossible possible: he shows the same couple for a second time, as if in a double take. Why do you think Monet might have done this?

A dark line of trees stretches across the horizon, giving the scene depth and variety. One tree looms higher, connecting the sky to the land.

Mont Sainte-Victoire

by Paul Cézanne (1839–1906)

Paul Cézanne has often been called "the father of modern art," because the developments in painting that he made in his lifetime influenced many artists at the beginning of the 20th century.

Like the Impressionist painters, with whom he sometimes exhibited, Cézanne worked outdoors. But he wanted to create a more permanent

type of art than their images of fleeting moments. By painting landscape with patches of shaped color Cézanne created scenes that looked solid, but which seemed at the same time full of movement.

Cézanne found that by laying warm colors, such as red or orange, next to cooler blues or greens, he could create a sense of depth. Can you see how the warmer colors jump forward from the canvas and appear nearer to your eye, while the cooler ones seem to be further away?

Painters had always used this technique in painting, but usually only on small parts of the canvas—not throughout an entire picture. Cézanne's new technique created a kind of optical illusion in which the viewer could at the same time see both a flat surface and one of great depth.

Cézanne painted the mountain of Sainte-Victoire, which was near his home in Provence in southern France, at least 60 times. Each time he found something new to depict in the majestic and enduring mountain landscape.

The Twentieth Century

Modern artists have searched for exciting new ways to express the different qualities they have found in the natural world and their personal feelings about it.

The optimism that greeted the modern age at the turn of the century led to an explosion of artistic styles and viewpoints in the years before the First World War began in 1914. Painters continued to meet together and form groups, as they had in previous centuries. But the emphasis in this century has been on the artist as an individual.

Landscapes of the mind

As in earlier centuries artists have been stimulated by science and ideas. One influence has been the exploration of the inner workings of the mind, or psychology. At the beginning of the century the pioneer of psychoanalysis, the Austrian Sigmund Freud, wrote about why people behaved in certain ways. He believed he could understand people by looking into their dreams. His ideas shocked many people but interested others, including the artist Gustav Klimt.

Klimt came from the same city as Freud, Vienna, the capital of Austria. Landscape was important to him. Every summer he would visit the lakes near his home and paint the countryside. In *Birch Wood* Klimt creates a rich pattern of golden reds for the fallen leaves and cool gray-blues for the tree trunks which has the feeling of a dream.

In Rubens's time, painters had tried to depict the simple life of the country in contrast to the teeming cities (*see page 19*). Now, by train or later by car, almost everyone could visit the countryside. This was good for the city dweller but brought new problems for the artist. How could he or she show the landscape in a way that seemed fresh to people who spent their weekends or vacations walking in it?

New ways of seeing

Some artists, such as the Russian Wassily Kandinsky (*see page 43*), tried to paint in an abstract way, so that the features of the landscape were represented by patches of color or lines. Artists wanted to say more about the landscape than just what it looked like. They did not try to show a realistic view in which the subject could be recognized: the camera could do this now. So they experimented with a huge variety of different techniques

Birch Wood: Gustav Klimt
Klimt does not try to show the trees in a realistic way but creates a decorative picture made up of colors, like a mosaic.

in order to create an original way of looking at the natural world.

Painters conveyed their feelings for nature through color and shape, telling us more about this feeling than the scene before them. At first many people could not identify with this challenging approach. But in time many came to enjoy the new visual experience, and found that paintings depicted nature in far more personal and suggestive ways than a photograph ever could.

The Sun

by Edvard Munch (1863–1944)

A village stands at the water's edge surrounded by dark, moss-covered rocks in a steep Scandinavian coastal valley, or fjord. For several months the weak winter sun has been too low in the sky for its rays to climb over the rocks and reach the villagers. Suddenly the day comes in spring when the bright sun rises high in the sky and bathes the valley in its warm glow.

This is the effect that Edvard Munch's huge mural, or wall painting would probably have had on its Norwegian audience. In their dark northern climate, this painting represented the life-giving force of the sun. Can you imagine how they might have reacted when they first saw it?

From a brilliant white center, dashes of paint in bright colors shoot out like sparks and fill the landscape with light. Look at the vivid streaks of greens, pinks, and blues that seem to shimmer and dazzle your eyes. Munch aimed to show that, however difficult or depressing life might be, the sun still has the power to heal.

From the age of about 30, Munch lived mainly in Germany but spent his summers in Norway. When he returned to his beloved homeland for good 17 years later, Munch settled in the coastal town of Kragerø, where he painted several pictures of its rough, windswept scenery. When he painted this image, he was already an established artist. In 1911, he won a prestigious competition for decorating the Great Hall of Oslo University. This was the largest, central panel of a whole series of murals he painted.

Munch's interest in painting large murals stemmed from his desire for as many people as possible to see his paintings. But Munch was also a very private person. He spent his last years on his own, living a poor and lonely life, surrounded only by his paintings, which he called his "children." Despite this affectionate name he treated his works badly. He scattered his prints all over the floor and hung out his paintings on apple trees to dry.

Many of Munch's paintings are pessimistic, but this one is an entirely positive image of renewal and natural energy. The year before he painted this mural he had suffered a nervous breakdown and his work reflected his depression. As he recovered, his paintings became more joyful. Many of them reflect both a renewed love of the landscapes of Norway and an interest in the lives of the ordinary people of his northern homeland.

The Turning Road, L'Estaque

by André Derain (1880–1954)

It is difficult to imagine today the impact this painting made on someone seeing it for the first time in 1906. Although artists had constantly tried to find new ways of recording nature, it was not until the early 20th century that they felt free to paint an object in whatever color they chose. Now, instead of green and brown, a tree could be red or even blue. Look how the French painter André Derain used such colors in this picture. He wanted to create a liveliness and impact that he thought was missing from the work of Impressionist painters such as Claude Monet.

An art critic who saw the work of Derain and similar artists at an exhibit was stunned by the brilliance of the colors and the free handling of paint. He remarked that the works must have been painted by "*fauves*," French for wild beasts. The name stuck—the painters became known as the Fauves.

Can you see what the figures are doing in this painting? Do they seem relaxed or active? Look at the man on the right struggling under the weight of a heavy jug. And have you noticed the figure traveling on a horse and cart across the bridge?

The way that Derain has placed colors next to each other makes them compete for attention. What do these clashing colors suggest to you? Do they create a calm and restful landscape, or one that is full of energy?

Although the painting is dazzlingly bright, Derain composed it in a careful way. Look closely. The picture seems to be made up of primary colors— red, yellow, and blue. But the red, the most prominent color, is actually made up of patches of orange, pink, and crimson. The dark blue and mauve of the pine trees in the background and the cool mauve-gray of the path at the bottom of the picture tone down the brightness. Can you see how this helps to balance the picture?

Look back at Monet's *Poppy Field* (*see page 33*) or Cézanne's *Mont Sainte-Victoire (see page 35)* and then look at this painting again. How are they different? Can you see how each artist applies the paint in a different way? In Derain's picture, much of the color is laid on in flat patches, held in place by thick curving lines. In other areas, it seems to shift and merge before your eyes. The painting vibrates with color and celebrates Derain's love of nature.

Train in Murnau

by Wassily Kandinsky (1866–1944)

Imagine traveling on a fast-moving train and looking through the window at the brightly lighted landscape. The exact shapes of the fields and hedges blur into a mass of different colors.

This painting of the Murnau landscape in southern Germany catches both the sensation of traveling at speed and the thrill of watching a train hurtling by. But Kandinsky does not try to create a strict sense of order. Can you see how he gives the picture depth by showing the clouds, thick blobs of paint, getting smaller as they recede? And, like earlier painters, he shows dark towering trees around which a lighter sky draws you into the distance.

On the left Kandinsky shows smoke puffing out of the chimneys of a village. In the bottom left-hand corner a blond girl in a red dress waves a white handkerchief at the train. Perhaps she knows the driver or one of the passengers, or maybe she is just waving in excitement.

The Russian-born painter Kandinsky spent the summers painting in the pretty village of Murnau until the First World War broke out in 1914. Often other painters would come and stay with him there. From the window of his cottage Kandinsky could see the houses of the village, the parish church, and the railroad. He used this scene several times in paintings. The artist was also influenced by the paintings on glass that he saw in Murnau, where they were still made in a traditional way. Though simple, these paintings were very expressive, with luminous, glowing colors.

When a painting is "abstract," it means that it is made up purely of colors and shapes, without a recognizable subject. Can you see how the artist is heading toward this way of painting in *Train at Murnau*? You can still recognize certain objects such as the shape of the train and the telegraph poles, so it is not entirely abstract. But can you see how it is the color and the shapes that really create the drama and movement in this painting rather than a realistic depiction of a speeding train? More and more, Kandinsky relied on vibrant colors to convey strong emotion.

A year after he painted this picture, in 1910, Kandinsky created his first completely abstract work. He turned away from representing the natural world around him. Instead he found a new means of expressing his vision and feelings in paint.

GLOSSARY

abstract art: art that does not represent objects or people that can be recognized in the real world, but which expresses a thought, idea, or feeling through colors and shapes.

Baroque: a 17th and 18th century art movement that used elaborate and theatrical forms to appeal to the viewer's emotions.

classical art: the painting and sculpture of ancient Greece and Rome.

Cubism: a 20th-century painting style that showed the structure of things, often by displaying different views of the subject at the same time.

Expressionism: a style of art in which color and form are used to suggest moods and feelings rather than mimic what is seen.

fresco: a way of painting on walls in which color is applied straight onto a layer of wet plaster.

Futurism: an art movement that used new techniques to express the excitement and dynamism of the early 20th century.

Impressionism: a style of painting in which artists tried to capture the effects of light and the atmosphere of a scene.

Industrial Revolution: a period of rapid technological change in the early 19th century when many Western countries were transformed by new machines and industries.

medium: the material with which a work of art is created, such as pencil, oil, or watercolor.

Middle Ages: the period of European history that lasted from about the fifth to the 15th centuries.

naïve art: a name given to art produced by untrained artists who often do not use advanced techniques such as perspective.

naturalism: an approach to art in which everyday objects, places, and people are shown without trying to idealize their appearance.

oil paint: a type of paint that uses oils to bind together the color.

pastel: crayons made from chalk and powdered pigment, which smudge on paper.

perspective: a method of drawing used to create an illusion of depth in a flat picture, using lines that meet at a single spot on the horizon known as the "vanishing point."

portrait: a painting that gives a likeness of a person and often an insight into his or her personality.

primitivism: a type of art that uses the shapes and symbols of tribal cultures from, for example, Africa, South America, or Asia.

realism: an approach to art that sees even ugly and unhappy scenes as being suitable subjects for artists.

Reformation: a 16th-century religious movement that protested many of the ideas of the Catholic Church and established the Protestant faith.

Renaissance: the "rebirth" of classical ideas that began in 14th century Italy, lasted to the 17th century, and led to a flowering of the visual arts and literature.

Rococo: An art movement of the early 18th century that used a delicate, elegant, decorative style.

Romanticism: a 19th-century movement in art and literature that celebrated the exotic, passionate, and dangerous.

sketch: a rough or quick version of a picture, often produced as a trial-run for a more finished work.

still life: a drawing or painting of objects that cannot move by themselves, such as fruit and flowers.

Surrealism: a 20th-century art movement that combines odd images to express the irrational and subconscious world of dreams or fantasy.

technique: the way an artist uses his or her materials.

watercolor: a type of paint in which colors dissolve in water.

looking at art
SET INDEX

FURTHER READING

Cummings, Pat, ed. *Talking with Artists*. Bradbury, 1992.

Greenberg, Jan, and Jordan, Sandra. *The Painter's Eye: Learning to Look at Contemporary Art*. Delacorte, 1991.

Isaacson, Philip M. *A Short Walk Around the Pyramids & Through the World of Art*. Knopf, 1993.

Janson, H.W. *History of Art*. Harry N. Abrams, Inc., 1995.

Powell, Jillian. *Painting and Sculpture*. Steck-Vaughn, 1990.

Sills, Leslie. *Visions: Stories about Women Artists*. Albert Whitman, 1993.

Testa, Fulvio. *If You Take a Paintbrush: A Book of Colors*. Dial, 1983.

Waterford, Giles. *Faces*. Atheneum, 1982.

Woolf, Felicity. *Picture This: A First Introduction to Paintings*. Doubleday, 1990

Yenawine, Philip. *Colors*. Delacorte, 1991; *Lines*. Delacorte, 1991; *Shapes*. Delacorte, 1991.

Zadrzynska, Ewa. *The Girl with a Watering Can*. Chameleon, 1990.

All details are taken from credited main pictures.
4: *Fresco from the Garden Room of Livia's Villa*. Photograph Bridgeman Art Library. 5: *Journey of the Magi*, Benozzo Gozzoli. Palazzo Medici-Riccardi, Florence/AKG London. 7: *Emperor Ming Huang's Journey to Shu*, Anonymous, 8th century. National Palace Museum, Taipei, Taiwan, Republic of China. 9: *Good Government in the Country*, Ambrogio Lorenzetti. Palazzo Pubblico, Siena/F. Lensini, Siena/Bridgeman Art Library. 11: *Madonna and Chancellor Rolin*, Jan van Eyck. Musée du Louvre, Paris/AKG London. 13: *Saint Francis in the Desert*, Giovanni Bellini. © The Frick Collection, New York. 15: *Rest on the Flight to Egypt*, Lucas Cranach. Staatlichte Museen zu Berlin/Bridgeman Art Library. 17: *Fall of Icarus*, Pieter Brueghel. Musées Royaux des Beaux-Arts, Brussels/Bridgeman Art Library. 18: *Jewish Cemetery*, Jacob van Ruisdael. Dresden Gemäldegalerie/AKG London. 19: *Landscape with Het Steen*, Peter Paul Rubens. National Gallery London/Bridgeman Art Library. 21: *Hagar and the Angel*, Claude Lorrain. National Gallery London/AKG London. 23: *Mr and Mrs Andrews*, Thomas Gainsborough. National Gallery London/AKG London. 25: *Blind Man's Buff*, Jean-Honoré Fragonard. Kress Collection, Washington DC/Bridgeman Art Library. 26: *The Traveler*, Caspar David Friedrich. Kunsthalle, Hamburg/AKG London. 27: *The Cornfield*, Vincent van Gogh. Private Collection/AKG London. 29: *The Haywain*, John Constable. National Gallery London/Bridgeman Art Library. 31: *Norham Castle*, J.M.W. Turner. Tate Gallery, London/Bridgeman Art Library. 33: *Poppy Field*, Claude Monet. Musée d'Orsay/AKG London. 35: *Mont Sainte-Victoire*, Paul Cézanne. Buhrle Collection, Zurich/Bridgeman Art Library. 36: *Trees: Buchenwald*, Gustav Klimt. Galerie im Belvedere, Vienna/AKG London. 39: *The Sun*, Edvard Munch. © The Munch Museum/The Munch-Ellingsen Group/DACS 1996. Photograph AKG London. 41: *The Turning Road*, André Derain. Oil on canvas, 1906, 51 x 76.75 inches, The Museum of Fine Arts, Houston; The John A. and Audrey Jones Beck Collection, © ADAGP, Paris and DACS, London 1996. 43: *Train in Murnau*, Wassily Kandinsky. © ADAGP, Paris and DACS, London 1996. Bridgeman Art Library.